WRITING ABOUT VILLAINS

by
Rayne Hall

Copyright Rayne Hall © 2013-2015

All Rights Reserved - content copyright Rayne Hall

Cover Art and Design by Erica Syverson

November 2015 Edition

Rayne Hall. St. Leonards.

ISBN-13: 978-1519356406

ISBN-10: 1519356404

CONTENTS

INTRODUCTION 5
CHAPTER 1: ARCHETYPES OF EVIL 6
CHAPTER 2: PINPOINTING THE ARCHETYPE 16
CHAPTER 3: GOAL, MOTIVATION AND MEANS 19
CHAPTER 4: THE PSYCHOLOGICAL PROFILE 24
CHAPTER 5: HERO AND VILLAIN ARE ALIKE 29
CHAPTER 6: THE VILLAIN'S GOOD SIDE 32
CHAPTER 7: REAL-LIFE INSPIRATION 35
CHAPTER 8: THE VILLAIN'S LAIR 37
CHAPTER 9: HENCHMEN AND MINIONS 41
CHAPTER 10: THE FINAL SHOWDOWN 47
CHAPTER 11: DIALOGUE AND TONE OF VOICE 49
CHAPTER 12: HANDS AND CLAWS 52
CHAPTER 13: SCARY SMILES 54
CHAPTER 14: HEROES AND VILLAINS - SOME DEFINITIONS 56
CHAPTER 15: CLICHES TO AVOID 60
CHAPTER 16: MEET KIRRAL, THE VILLAIN OF STORM DANCER 65
DEAR READER 75

INTRODUCTION

I love villains.

Forget the cardboard evil-doers with their evil laughter and stinking breath. Your villains will have personality, ideals, feelings and conflicts. They will challenge your heroes, chill your readers, and give your novel excitement and depth. This book shows you how to create fiends whom readers love to hate and can't forget.

In the first chapters, we'll look at characterisation, tapping into the power of archetypes without stereotyping, making your villains fearsome, believable and unique. Then we explore writing techniques. Simple yet effective sentences can bring your fiend to life and make the readers' skin crawl.

You can use this book to create a new villain for a future novel, or to flesh out the one from your current work in progress.

The techniques work for most stories, whether you write a romance, an urban fantasy, a thriller, a horror novel or a children's book. You are the CEO of your writing; you decide which of my suggestions you use where and how.

In some sections, I've used 'she' and in others 'he', and I've employed the words 'hero' and 'villain' for women and men alike. Almost everything in this book applies to either gender.

I'm using British words, spellings, grammar and punctuation.

Enjoy creating the kind of villain your novel deserves.

Rayne Hall

CHAPTER 1: ARCHETYPES OF EVIL

Certain types of characters have played a role in storytelling since humans discovered language. They appear again and again, always recognisable, yet always different. They resonate with the reader's subconscious on a deep level.

The archetype is an important part of the villain's characterisation - but it's not a substitute for proper character development. Unless fleshed out as individuals, archetypes remain lifeless.

Here are the ten archetypes. If you're starting a new work of fiction, choose the one that intrigues you, and use it as the basis for the characterisation. If your story is already in progress, you'll probably recognise your villain's character in one of the ten archetypes. It will 'click' and feel right. Use it to deepen the character.

Although I've used 'he' for some and 'she' for others, these archetypes apply to either gender.

TEN VILLAIN ARCHETYPES

1. The Evil Overlord

This villain sits at the top of a power pyramid and wants still more power: king, slave owner, gangster boss, prison director, boarding school headmaster, convent abbess, care home matron, controlling patriarch, wife batterer, CEO, political dictator, alpha of werewolf clan. He is most often found in historical and fantasy fiction.

He is motivated by power and control. His aim is to keep and expand his empire.

His style is based on long-term planning. He plots years and decades ahead, and always keeps the big picture in mind. He is extremely intelligent, and his decisions are rapid and ruthless. He gets other people to support his goals. To keep his minions in line, he uses the carrot and the stick - a blend of incentives and threats. He has no scruples manipulating others, and is skilled in subverting their noble ideals and religious convictions to evil. Sometimes he masterminds several other villains.

Either he came from a humble and hopeless position (perhaps he was an abused orphan, or a monarch's illegitimate son) and plotted his way to the top - or was a selfless hero who courageously led the people in the struggle against oppression until the fight was won, when he became the new ruler and his new power corrupted him.

He fears only one thing: to lose control. His weakness is a distrust of his followers; he may suspect traitors everywhere and have his most loyal henchmen executed on suspicion of treason.

2. The Schemer

This villain fits into any society and any fiction genre. She may be the heroine's sister, neighbour, colleague or friend. She may be the efficient secretary who trades the company's secrets to the competition, the double agent selling information to rival nations, or the counsellor who poisons the client's mind. In some works of fiction, she's not the arch villain, but a minor villain, and her villainy may not be revealed until the novel's Black Moment.

Her plans are for the long term. She identifies people who can help her attain her goal, and sets out to befriend them. She does them favours, supports them, gains their trust, and makes them believe that she's their friend.

She is motivated by ambition. Whether she wants to achieve a senior management job, steal another woman's husband, become the most popular girl in class or marry a millionaire, she knows what she wants and schemes to get it. Even those closest to her have no idea what she's really after. She appears trustworthy.

Sometimes, she is secretly afraid that she won't measure up.

Her weakness may be an unawareness of how other people are scheming. She doesn't have the same grasp on the big picture as the Evil Overlord has, and may learn too late that for all her clever planning, she was just a pawn in someone else's game. Sometimes, this villain's downfall is a trap she has set for others.

3. The Obsessed Scientist

This villain is intelligent, analytical, creative and determined. He may be a computer hacker, magician, alchemist, inventor, researcher, professor, doctor or engineer. In some works of fiction, he's presented as a 'mad scientist' but more often, he's frighteningly sane.

He is popular in thrillers, steampunk and science fiction.

His goal is to prove to the world, and especially to his peers, that he is right, that his hypothesis, his invention, his solution works. He needs this acknowledgement.

His style is analytical and focused. He'll do what it takes to achieve his goal, and if necessary, he'll make great personal sacrifices.

All his life, no one took him seriously. His classmates in school viewed him as a nerd. Later, his peers mocked his theories. Professional organisations may have refused to admit him as a member, or may have disqualified him or kicked him out - unfairly, in his opinion. Now he's going to show them.

His means to bring about the desired result are unscrupulous. Often, they involve cruel experiments on animals or on human prisoners. His conscience has no problem with killing, maiming and tormenting others for the cause. Since he's willing to make sacrifices, he doesn't see why others shouldn't make sacrifices, too.

He may have a sadistic streak and enjoy tormenting his study subjects.

His weakness is hubris. He is so convinced of his superior intelligence, so desperate to show it off, and so keen to prove that his invention works that a skilled manipulator can lead him into a trap.

4. The Smothering Mother

This villain dominates her family - or her community or club. She will do anything for them, and in return, expects unquestioned loyalty, love and obedience. She commands and lies.

She is motivated by the need to control others.

She expects every member of her family to obey her, and punishes those who deviate from her will by moving into their own apartment without her permission, or by marrying a person she did not approve of. She knows she's right, and she demands total obedience from everyone for their own good.

In return, she'll protect and defend them. She believes her darlings to be perfect - except when they disobey - and denies or justifies their mistakes. Her darling son is a serial rapist? It's the women's fault. Her sweet daughter murdered a child? Impossible. The Smothering Mother will provide a fake alibi and swear every oath that her daughter did not leave her side.

The Smothering Mother's downfall occurs when members of her family turn against her.

5. The Fanatic

This villain is motivated by deeply held - often religious - convictions. He's certain that God wants him to slaughter unbelievers, torture suspected witches, burn heretics at the stake and force conversions at sword-point. He's perfect for historical fiction and some types of thrillers. He may be a cult leader, conqueror, inquisitor, prophet, priest, crusader, suicide bomber or terrorist.

His beliefs are genuine, and that's what makes him so dangerous. Reasoning with him is pointless, because no argument holds up against what he thinks is the will of God. He may also have the support of others who share his faith, either individuals or a large network, and this makes it difficult for anyone to stand up to him.

The fanatic fears neither pain nor death. Indeed, he may welcome it, since he believes that dying while doing 'God's work' guarantees him a place in heaven. The only thing he fears is failing God by not delivering the required body count.

He may do genuine good deeds - work tirelessly to care for the sick and wounded, pay for the education of orphans, protect battered wives from abuse - because that's also part of his religious duty.

This villain has a strong sense of honour - but it is different from what you, the hero, or the reader consider honourable.

His narrow mindedness can bring about his downfall. He may be so focused on his cause that he doesn't realise how the Evil Overlord is manipulating him - and the Evil Overlord has no scruples about executing a Fanatic who has outlasted his use. Sometimes, a Fanatic unleashes a machinery of religious persecution and then gets caught up in it himself, especially when another Fanatic declares his beliefs to be heretical.

6. The Seductress

This villain works well in romance and historical fiction. She may be a love rival, a courtesan or a spy.

She uses her charms - either her body or her mind - to get what she wants. Whether she plays the innocent to persuade the dying millionaire to adopt her, sleeps with a politician to trick him into divulging state secrets, or simply listens so attentively that her flattered victim can't help but fall in love and divorce his wife for her, she makes people feel good so that they grant her her desire.

This archetype's motivation is not clear-cut. Often, there's an underlying need for security, or a need to bolster her self-esteem.

She is good at sizing people up, street-smart, manipulative, and a liar. She does not feel sorry for those she harmed - not for the wife whose husband she stole, not for the children she orphaned, not for the politician ousted from office after the affair comes out. She cares only about herself.

7. The Sadist

This villain is wonderful for thrillers, especially in the role of a serial killer. He targets specific victims - for example, teenage prostitutes or homeless men - and torments them.

His motivation is pleasure, often tinged with erotic arousal. He gets a thrill from his victims' pain or fear. Sometimes, there's a religious element involved - he believes God has called him to punish prostitutes - but the main motivation is the pursuit of thrills.

He is exceptionally intelligent, takes risks and fears nothing. Sometimes, he taunts his pursuers, e.g. by giving the police clues about his identity, or by insinuating himself into an investigation. The Sadist villain may be a sociopath.

Often, the Sadist leads a double life. When he's not dismembering children, he may be a tender husband, doting father, pious worshipper and pillar of society.

He probably experienced continuous cruel violence as a child, and may have practised abuse against other children or against animals at a young age.

8. The Confidence Trickster

Charm is this villain's trademark. She is good at reading people, adaptable, confident, persuasive, inspiring. She tricks people into giving up their life savings, buying worthless stocks, and changing their wills in her favour. Often, she uses other people's own moral weaknesses to lure them into a trap.

She may be a con artist, a card sharp, an internet scammer, an impersonator. Most often, she completes one scam and immediately plans the next, bigger one.

Her motivation is greed. She wants something - usually wealth - and she feels that because she wants it, she's entitled to it. She doesn't respect other people's rights.

Her fear is poverty.

In her childhood, she may have suffered deprivation because her parents were gullible, and she swore this would not happen to her. She chose to become a scammer instead of a victim.

She may detest violence, and avoid hurting her victims physically - but she has no qualms about leaving them helpless and starving.

Her downfall is usually her arrogance. She may pull off bigger and bigger scams, over-confident in her ability. Some of her victims may not be as gullible as they seemed.

9. The Social Reject

This villain is outside society. He may have been formally cast out, or people may shun him for a specific reason, or perhaps he's simply not likeable. He may be the outlaw, the nerd, the misfit, or simply the unpopular boy in class.

His back story may create reader sympathy. He may have been cast out or shunned because of a physical disability, a disfiguring facial mark, his ethnicity, his caste or his illegitimate birth. Perhaps he was once favoured and then discarded - for example, when his mother remarried and gave all her love to her new children - or he may always have been treated as being worth less than the others - for example, the king's younger son. Whatever happened, he resented it deeply, and he still nurtures his hurt.

As an outsider, he is often the scapegoat for other people's misdeeds. Whether a murder has been committed or valuables have vanished, he's automatically the suspect. This increases his resentment and reduces his scruples. If he gets blamed for bad stuff, he'll give them bad stuff.

He is motivated by a yearning for love or for acceptance, either by society, or by a specific person or group, although he may deny this longing.Sometimes, this villain is also motivated by a craving for vengeance, as he wants to pay back those who hurt him.

His style is street smart, intuitive, and occasionally charismatic. He's a keen observer and often understands human nature well, but despite his perceptiveness, he lacks the social skills to fit in.

His weakness is his emotion. He feels everything deeply. His judgement is clouded by hatred and resentment, and he misses opportunities because of his pessimism and bitterness. In critical situations, he may not be in control of his emotions.

This villain works well especially in urban fantasy, westerns, and YA.

In some works of fiction, this villain redeems himself and finds his way back into society. Sometimes, he sacrifices himself. For example, he may die to give the heroine a chance to escape from the Evil Overlord.

10. The Bully

This villain picks vulnerable victims, such as social outcasts, unpopular classmates, lonely hearts, mentally ill or physically disabled people, members of ethnic minorities. He may be the bully in high school, or he may be a cyber-troll who finds his victims in forums on the internet.

He is motivated by the short term power boost his ego gets when he holds power over a victim.

He seizes opportunities rather than pursue a long-term strategy. Unlike some other villain archetypes, the Bully doesn't necessarily have superior intelligence. He's good at manipulating people, but only in certain situations. He has a bag of techniques for making vulnerable people helpless.

His greatest fear is being bullied himself. Often, he's a coward at heart.

His downfall is that he doesn't inspire loyalty. He may have minions, but those support him only while he's dominant and strong. Once he loses a fight, his followers desert him. He also risks that one of his lieutenants grows into a superior bully and ousts him from his leadership role.

This villain works well in short stories and in YA fiction. If you want to pitch two villains against one another, have the Bully pick a seemingly easy victim... who turns out to be the Social Reject.

DEFYING EXPECTATIONS

Although some of these archetypes are common in one gender, e.g. the Evil Overlord and the Bully are usually male, while the Smothering Mother and the Seductress are mostly female, you can cast them in either gender. This creates an original, fresh effect.

Surprise the reader further by choosing an archetype they didn't expect in the context. What if the villainous king isn't an Evil Overlord but a Smothering Mother? What if the head of the research programme isn't an Obsessed Scientist but a Confidence Trickster?

Feel free to deviate from the archetype and make it fit your villain's character. However, the more closely you stick to the archetype, the stronger it will resonate with the reader.

ARCHETYPE VERSUS STEREOTYPE

The archetype is a character model that is timeless and universal. All over the world, throughout human history, these archetypes have enriched stories. They are part of the 'collective unconscious', the awareness all humans share. By tapping into the creative unconscious, you can create a deep resonance.

The stereotype is a character who is so similar to other characters that he might have been shaped by the same cookie cutter. This often comes from the expectation that all characters of a certain kind have the same personality. Stereotypical characters are flat like cardboard cut-outs, predictable and boring.

Using archetypes is good; using stereotypes is bad. Yet archetypes can easily become stereotypes if you don't develop them. Don't use the naked archetypes, but use your creativity to clothe them with values, strengths, weaknesses, passions, desires, habits and quirks.

ASSIGNMENT

Choose an archetype for your villain. Surprisingly often, writers reading description of the archetypes immediately recognise their villain in one of them. If you're uncertain, narrow your choice to two or three possibilities. Chapter 2 will help you make the best choice.

CHAPTER 2: PINPOINTING THE ARCHETYPE

Most writers, when reading the profiles of the archetypes, know immediately which of them suits the villain type they have in mind.

However, it's not always so easy and obvious. After narrowing the list down to two or three possibilities, you may feel stuck. Here are comparisons between archetypes whose features overlap.

The Sadist or the Bully?

Both enjoy power over victims. While the Sadist gets a sexual thrill, the Bully gains a temporary boost of self-esteem. The Sadist's intelligence is great, while the Bully's may be average. The Sadist selects a specific victim type and thrives on a challenge, while the Bully preys on easy victims. The Sadist is fearless; the Bully is a coward at heart.

The Bully or the Evil Overlord?

Both like power and control. The Bully seizes opportunities; while the Evil Overlord plans far ahead, The Bully enjoys power of the moment, while the Evil Overlord pursues a big goal.The Evil Overlord is skilled at manipulating all kinds of people under any circumstances, whereas the Bully is good at manipulating only weak, frightened people in specific situations. The Bully does not have the Evil Overlord's superior intelligence and long-term strategies.

The Smothering Mother or the Evil Overlord?

Both rule and control their empire, and both have long-term strategies. The Smothering Mother is emotional and passionate. The Evil Overlord is unemotional, calm, and without scruples. The Smothering

Mother genuinely believes that what she wants is in the best interest of the people she rules, while the Evil Overlord only pretends to believe it; he acts for his own good. Unlike the Evil Overlord's, the Smothering Mother's need for control is personal. Rather than expanding an empire, she wants only the best for her family. Where the Smothering Mother is passionate and warm, the Evil Overlord is ruthless and cold. Her decisions are painful and slow; his are cold and quick.

If a strategy fails, the Smothering Mother can't believe that her beautiful scheme hasn't worked. The Evil Overlord simply switches to Plan B. The Smothering Mother may be blind to her offspring's fault, while the Evil Overlord knows all his subordinates' weaknesses and strengths. The Smothering Mother may trust her lieutenants too much, while the Evil Overlord may distrust his to the point of paranoia.

The Smothering Mother is usually female while the Evil Overlord is more often male, although this is not always the case.

The Schemer or the Confidence Trickster?

Both are skilled manipulators and trick other people for gain. The Schemer is motivated by ambition, the Confidence Trickster by greed. The Schemer pursues a long-term goal while the Confidence Trickster prefers quick gains.

Mixing Archetypes

If you're still uncertain, you may be tempted to make your villain a hodgepodge of archetypes. However, the pure archetypes resonate strongest within the reader's subconscious.

Choose just one archetype for your villain's core, and use elements from the others as embellishments.

If in doubt, identify the archetype by motivation, because the motivation is at his core. The motivation leads to the goal, the goal leads to the means.

As your villain matures and gains experience, he will widen his repertoire of means and add new strategies and tricks, and you can borrow those from the other archetypes - but at the core, he will remain the same.

ASSIGNMENT

Decide which archetype is at your villain's core. It's best to make this decision early, before you do further work.

CHAPTER 3: GOAL, MOTIVATION AND MEANS

A villain who is evil for evil's sake is boring, and the readers will forget him as soon as they've finished the book. To give your story excitement and make your villain memorable, give him a clear goal and strong motivation.

The goal is what the villain wants.

The motivation is why he wants it.

The means is how he goes about getting it.

Make the goal as clear as possible, and the motivation as strong as possible.

Goal and Motivation Examples

Goal: *To be the richest man in France*

Motivation: *To pamper his mother after a lifetime of deprivation*

Goal: *To be the richest man in France*

Motivation: *To afford the most beautiful collection of antique clocks*

Goal: *To be the richest man in France*

Motivation: *To be able to buy wildlife habitats threatened by industrial development*

Goal: *To appease his bloodthirsty goddess with child sacrifices*

Motivation: *To prolong his own life (the goddess grants him one day per sacrificed child)*

Goal: *To appease his bloodthirsty goddess with child sacrifices*

Motivation: *To prolong his little son's life (the goddess grants him one day per sacrificed child)*

Goal: *To kill as many heathens as possible.*

Motivation: *To impress his king and gain power.*

Goal: *To kill as many heathens as possible.*

Motivation: *To gain guaranteed entry into his religion's paradise.*

Goal: To *kill as many heathens as possible.*

Motivation: *To avenge his family who were slaughtered by heathens.*

The means - how he goes about achieving this - may change during the story. At first, they may be honourable, but then they become increasingly ruthless and gruesome.

The man who wants to be the richest man in France may have started out with hard work, then increasingly made use of opportunities, then created opportunities at the expense of others, then he deliberately exploited others' weaknesses, then cheated others. Now he is at the stage where he sets out to ruin rich people, and before the novel's end, he'll murder to get more money.

ADD A NOBLE ELEMENT

To give your story depth, give your villain's goal or motivation an element of nobility.

He may have noble ideals. The goal he works for may be something the reader applauds, and the motivation something the reader understands... but the means he uses to achieve his goal are horrific.

This technique works better for some archetypes than for others. If your villain is a Smothering Mother or an Evil Overlord, you can probably find a strong noble element in their goal and motivation, because they genuinely want the best for their family or their country. The Obsessed Scientist may aim to save an endangered species, and the Fanatic to save souls.

With other archetypes, this may not work as easily, especially with the Sadist and the Bully who seek cruelty for pleasure's sake.

If you can add a noble element to your villain's goal or motivation, go for it, because it gives your story depth.

WHEN NOBILITY BECOMES TWISTED

Often, the villain's goal and motivation are pure and noble, but the means he uses are villainous. This is often the case with the Obsessed Scientist who'll do anything to achieve his noble goal and shuts his eyes to the suffering he causes. To save an endangered species from extinction, he'll torture hundreds of laboratory animals. To find a cure for cancer, he carries out lethal experiments on children.

Other villains have a noble goal, but interpret it in shocking ways. Take Adolf Hitler, whose goal was to lead the German nation to glory - a noble goal in a politician or ruler, which initially gained him many followers. But his vision of 'glory' differed from that of most people, involving a single-race nation under a totalitarian government. The means he used to achieve this goal - extermination of non-Aryans and political opponents, concentration camps, total war - were definitely those of a villain.

Writing About Villains

Many true-life villains of the Evil Overlord type started out as genuine noble heroes and rulers. Once they gained power, they used it to secure and increase their power, and this led to an ever-increasing spiral of power abuse. Historic examples include the Roman Emperors Tiberius and Nero who started as benevolent rulers before they became corrupted by power, and Mao Zedong (Mao Tse Tung) the inspiring heroic leader of the Chinese Revolution who, once in power, unleashed a mad wave of destruction and terror upon his people.

The villain may have started out with a noble goal, a noble motivation, and even noble means - and gradually become evil.

Perhaps a woman's child is dying and can only be saved with a kidney transplant. There are no suitable donor kidneys available... except one, and that person, although fatally injured in an accident and in a coma, is still alive. The person will die the next day - too late for the child. If the person died today, the child would be saved. After considering the ethical dilemma, the woman switches off the life support, so the person dies, the transplant happens and her child is saved. Is this morally wrong? It depends on your ethics. Is it evil? No.

But then, the transplanted kidney fails. Once again, the child needs a new kidney or will die. No matching kidney is available. There is one potential donor - an idle bum who exploits the welfare system. He is depressed and wants to kill himself. So she encourages the suicide. The kidney becomes available, her child lives. Is she right in doing this? She has crossed the line to what most people consider murder. Although readers will still sympathise with her motivation (to save her child), most will no longer approve of the means.

The child needs expensive follow-up surgery, and she can't afford it. What now? She knows how much money good organs fetch, and she has experience in procuring them. She induces another potential suicide to kill himself, and sells his kidney. At this stage, although the motivation is still noble, the ruthlessness of her method makes her a villain.

The child's health remains delicate, and special schooling and support are expensive. The woman wants the best for her child, but cannot afford it. There's a black market for human organs, with wealthy people offering any price for kidneys, livers and hearts. Out in the street are those useless bums, the dregs of society, most of them criminals, good for nothing. She traps several and sells their bodies for organ harvesting. By now the reader's sympathies for her motivation dwindle and give way to a shudder about her means.

Next, the woman considers all those illegal immigrants whom nobody will miss. Hundreds of kidneys, hearts and livers, ready for the taking. As her organ-harvesting business grows, she lures more refugees from abroad to increase her supplies. She becomes rich and can afford a luxurious lifestyle for her beloved child and herself. At this stage, the once noble element of her motivation has given way to sheer evil.

The villain who gradually transcends boundaries is chilling for the reader, perfect for thrillers. However, this type is difficult to write. The author needs to decide what stage of development the villain has already reached at the beginning of the story, and find ways to incorporate the back story without creating an infodump.

ASSIGNMENT

Identify your villain's goal and motivation. Define them in short, simple sentences. The more clearly and precisely you can express them, the better. It will make your writing easier and more powerful. You may want to print out these sentences and stick them on your computer monitor, or copy and paste them into your villain's character profile. They're crucial. Keep to them and remember them.

Identify one or several means she uses to attain her goal. If you like, you can replace these with others later if better ideas arise during the writing.

CHAPTER 4: THE PSYCHOLOGICAL PROFILE

Get to know your villain as well as you know your heroes, and develop a full character profile for her. Certain characteristics are especially useful for fiction plots. Your villain should have most - though not necessarily all - of them.

1. Intelligent.

A highly intelligent villain makes a worthy adversary. The more intelligent the villain, the greater the challenge to find her out and bring her down. The villain's intelligence helps make the plot plausible and exciting. This is especially important in novels where the villain plays a major role, such as thrillers. The Evil Overlord, the Obsessed Scientist and the Sadist are often unusually intelligent; their IQ may be far above that of the average population. The Bully's intelligence is sometimes only average, but he's not stupid. Stupid villains make boring fiction, although they may work for subplots.

2. Psychologically astute.

The villain is skilled at reading, persuading and manipulating other people. The Schemer, the Seductress, the Confidence Trickster and the Evil Overlord are especially good at it. The Bully excels only in some forms of psychological manipulations. The Fanatic, the Obsessed Scientist and the Social Outcast may or may not possess great psychological skills.

3. Single-minded.

Neither temptations nor scruples distract the villain from her goal. Only the Bully can sometimes be distracted. The Obsessed Scientist is the most focused of them all. She won't deviate one inch. The Evil Overlord may show some flexibility, but this is simply her Plan B to achieve the same goal.

4. Good-looking.

If your villain is beautiful, handsome or sexy, she has a great advantage. With her flawless beauty, rugged handsomeness or glamorous appeal, she can easily gain people's attention and trust. A handsome man has little difficulty impersonating a hospital doctor or selling fake investments, and an angelic blue-eyed girl can convince others of her innocence. However, good looks are not a must. Your villain may be plain or ugly, and her ugliness may have made her bitter and contributed to her resentment. The Seductress and the Confidence Trickster probably possess great physical attractiveness. The Social Outcast, on the other hand, may be ugly, disfigured by illness or fate.

5. Popular.

People like the villain, follow her, support her. They love her so much that they'll swear any oath on her innocence and provide her with false alibis. This is either because they can't believe that their adored idol/lover/boss could be capable of evil, or because the villain has persuaded them that her evil is right. The more loyalty the villain inspires in her followers, the more difficult it is for the heroes to expose her and bring her down. The Evil Overlord is especially good at inspiring loyalty. People really believe this villain is their mentor, their friend, their supporter, and will do anything for her. The Obsessed Scientist may not have this popularity.

6. Trauma survivor.

Something dreadful happened to the villain when she was a child, probably some kind of continuous abuse. This contributed to her twisted personality. It gives the reader some sympathy for her - but not too much. A neat trick for creating story depth is to give the hero and the villain similar back stories. Both experienced the same trauma and were shaped by it, but made different choices. When the hero turned to the light, the villain turned to darkness. While the Social Outcast nurses his wound and is filled with resentment and plans for revenge, the Evil Overlord strives for a position where no one will ever be able to hurt him again.

7. Liar.

Lies and truths are tools for the villain, and she applies whichever is more useful at the moment. She lies fluently and convincingly, especially if she's a Confidence Trickster or a Schemer. The Social Outcast may disdain lies.

8. Suspicious.

The villain distrusts everyone, even her closest allies, to the point of paranoia. This trait is especially strong in the Social Outcast and in the Evil Overlord. Real-life Evil Overlords - such as Joseph Stalin - often execute their faithful followers by the hundreds, and sacrifice even their loyal lieutenants in paranoid purges.

9. Hubris.

She considers herself superior to other people. The Fanatic knows she's more righteous than the other followers of her religion, the Sadist knows she's cleverer than the police investigating her serial killing and the Obsessed Scientist knows she has more expertise than her colleagues. Even the Social Outcast has hubris: she feels that she has suffered more injustice than anyone else.

10. Self-centred.

What matters to the villain is what the villain needs or wants. Everything else is of secondary importance, if it matters at all. When others suffer, she considers how to use this to her own advantage, although she excels at faking sympathy. Only the Social Outcast sometimes feels genuine sympathy for others.

11. Ambitious.

The villain has a lofty goal and strives to attain it. It may be for herself - especially if she's an Evil Overlord or a Schemer - or on behalf of others - especially if she's a Smothering Mother. The Bully may lack this trait. Often, the villain's ambition increases during the story. Initially, the Evil Overlord seeks to rule a province, then she seeks to rule the country, and then the world. The Confidence Trickster aims to make a hundred bucks, then a thousand, then a million.

12. Unscrupulous.

For the villain, the end always justifies the means.

13. Enjoys challenges.

The villain is confident and seeks increasingly tough opponents and greater dangers, especially the Sadist.

14. Has a good side.

Give your story depth by creating a villain with a genuine good side. Perhaps she loves animals or children, and goes to great lengths to protect them. She may volunteer at an animal shelter, or risk her life to save a drowning child. If you want to create real dilemmas, let the villain save the hero's child. His obligation of gratitude may prevent him from moving against the villain fast enough, or may even delude him that the villain cannot possibly have done the terrible things attributed to her.

ASSIGNMENT

Choose which of these fourteen character traits apply to your villain. If uncertain, re-read the description of your chosen archetype. If in doubt, include the trait. Jot down some ideas in what way this trait is apparent.

CHAPTER 5: HERO AND VILLAIN ARE ALIKE

You can increase your novel's emotional impact by making the hero and the villain alike. Of course, they're very different - one is good, one is evil - but you can find and emphasise similarities. This gives the reader a deeper understanding of both, and adds an extra dimension to your story.

Here are some ideas. If you like, you can use several, although one or two may be enough.

1. SAME GOAL

If both pursue the same goal, this emphasises their different means. The hero's means are fair, the villain's foul. Perhaps both want to marry the same woman, both want to be the company's CEO, or both want to rule the land. This works especially well in the Chicklit and Fantasy genres. However, you need to decide it from the outset. Once you've written a draft, changing a major character's goal is difficult.

2. SAME MOTIVATION

Hero and villain have the same motivation, but they pursue different goals. This works well for character-driven fiction, literary fiction, and many forms of dark fiction, as well as for stories exploring different facets of a theme. For example, if your novel explores ambition, this may be the driving force for your villain and your hero, but it takes them in opposite directions. This type of novel often has great psychological depth. If you choose to give your villain the same motivation as your hero, consider a scene where the hero is tempted to pursue an evil goal or to use foul means. Perhaps she even succumbs to temptation, and for the rest of the story seeks to atone for her mistake.

3. SIMILAR POSITION IN SOCIETY

Perhaps both are barons, beggars or barristers. This levels the playing field and creates a fair challenge. It works especially well in novels where conflict between hero and villain is a subplot. It's less suitable for novels where the hero is an underdog on a quest to defeat the all-powerful villain.

4. SHARED ORIGINS

They belong to the same family or the same ethnic minority, were raised in the same slum or arrived as refugees from the same country.

5. SIMILAR BACKSTORY

Both are high school dropouts, illegal immigrants, or former Olympic medallists. If you're revising a nearly-finished novel, this is a similarity you may be able to insert without changing much of the plot.

6. SIMILAR WOUND

This one is potent. A traumatic event or similarity shaped both characters... but it inspired them to take different paths. Perhaps both were raised by neglectful, drug-addicted parents, both witnessed the slaughter of their families by the conquering army, both were betrayed by the person they loved, both were single parents at a young age, both grew up in the same abusive orphanage, or both were crippled in their youth by illness or violence.

This wound creates reader sympathy - but it also emphasises that the villain had a choice. While the trauma was a catalyst in her development, it did not force her to become evil. She could have chosen the path of light, like the hero did.

At one stage in the book, the revelation of the similar wound may raise the hero's (and the reader's) hopes that the two will find common ground, and that the villain will be converted to the light... and then you can dash those hopes in the next scene.

ASSIGNMENT

Choose one or several similarities between villain and hero.

CHAPTER 6: THE VILLAIN'S GOOD SIDE

Villains who are pure evil are boring. Readers soon forget those cardboard characters. Make your villains three-dimensional and memorable by giving them a good side.

I'm not talking about faked compassion or carefully planned tokens of philanthropy to impress others, but genuine goodness.

The villain has ideals and values of which the reader approves. There's something the villain really cares about besides herself and her goal. What is it? The clue may lie in your villain's archetype, or in your story's plot.

It may be something major, and it may be connected to the motivation. But it may also be something unrelated, and it can be bizarre.

Perhaps she cares about children, about animals, about the elderly, endangered species, the under-privileged or the disabled? Then she'll go to great lengths to help and protect them, not just with easy donations, but with a hands-on approach.

Here are some ideas. She may work tirelessly as a hospital volunteer, doing dogsbody work without complaining. Perhaps she devotes her free time to cleaning pens at the animal shelter, or to preparing meals at a soup kitchen. She may care deeply for stray cats and always put out a saucer of milk for them, or she helps protect an endangered butterfly species by creating a wildlife sanctuary in her garden. Maybe she provides pro bono legal advice or medical treatment for impoverished families, or sees to it that every school building in town is in good repair.

SHOW THE KINDNESS IN ACTION

Show the villain's good side in action; don't just tell the reader about it. Weave it into a live scene for the reader to witness. When other medics refuse to go near the plague victims for fear of infection, the villain devotes herself to treating those patients. Where others stand by and watch a boy drowning in the freezing lake, she jumps into the icy waters to save the child.

PLOT POTENTIAL

If your villain has a good side, this not only makes the villain more interesting, but it creates exciting plot possibilities.

What if the villain's genuine goodness is so widely known and admired that people simply cannot believe this saintly person to be capable of evil deeds? The investigating police officer practically knows she's the serial killer, but his boss tells him to stop harassing this saint.

What if the investigating police officer identifies this woman as the prime suspect... but then recognises her as the one who works selflessly in the hospital? He can't imagine her to be the evil villain, so he delays pursuing this trail until it's too late.

What if only one witness saw the perpetrator and could bring her to justice... but he won't testify against her, because she had been so kind to his mother dying in hospital?

What if the villain risked her life to rescue a child from a burning house... and the child is the hero's son? His gratitude will cloud his judgement or create an obligation. What if he witnesses the villain assaulting a victim, he has a gun, and the only way to stop the assault is to shoot the villain? What if he recognises his son's noble rescuer - and this makes him hesitate a moment too long? The assault happens, the victim dies, and the villain gets away.

ASSIGNMENT

Choose one genuinely good side for your villain character. How can you show it live in action? Is there a way you can use it to create a difficulty or dilemma for your hero? Although not every villain needs a good side, it will add depth to your novel if he does. If you're stuck for ideas, do some creative brainstorming exercises.

CHAPTER 7: REAL-LIFE INSPIRATION

The people who harmed or hurt you in real life provide wonderful material for your fiction. Use them as inspiration for your villains, and you'll get something positive out of the experience.

We all have had villains in our lives. You may still hurt from the wounds they caused or fume about their unfairness. Perhaps you're currently suffering from their selfishness and cruelty. If none comes to mind, here are some prompts to trigger your memory:

- Your brother who mutilated your pet, and then framed you for the deed, so your parents thought you were the cruel one.

- The religious leader who abused you and other children sexually in the confident knowledge that nobody would believe your words against his.

- Your violent ex-husband who beat you brutally, yet in public always claimed that he would never hurt a woman.

- The girl who pretended to be your best friend so she could steal your fiancé.

- The boss who worked you to exhaustion, dangling the carrot of promotion before you, but never kept his promise, and when you ruined your health in his service fired you without compensation.

- The racist teacher who didn't like the colour of your skin and got you excluded from the sports team that meant the world to you, by accusing you of something she knew you didn't do.

- The confidence trickster who swindled your ageing mum out of her retirement fund.

- The club member who slandered you and damaged your reputation irrevocably so he got elected on the committee in your place.

- The colleague who pretended to support your work but stole your ideas and passed them off as his own.

Make a list of the villains in your life, minor and major. For each, try to guess their goal and motivation. Their means - the methods by which they operated - are particularly interesting. How did they manage to manipulate, seduce, deceive, bully, victimise or abuse you? Why did you initially permit it or fall for it? When and how did you realise that they meant to harm you? Were you their only selected victim, or one of many? Did they gain pleasure from tormenting you, or were you simply a tool they used to get what they wanted?

Try to remember details of their behaviour: the sound of their voice, their gestures, speech patterns, manners and behaviourisms. Can any of these fit the villain in the story you're writing?

If you like, you can take this idea further. Instead of using just parts of this nasty person and adding them to a fictional character, you can base the villain fully on this person you know. However, be careful. If they recognise themselves, or are recognised by others, they may sue you for libel. Resist the temptation to use your novel to expose those people in public. Change important details such as gender and name.

You can also model your villain on historical personages. If your villain is an Evil Overlord, study the strategies of despots like Adolf Hitler and Josef Stalin. For Sadists, a serial killer like Jack the Ripper may be a useful model.

ASSIGNMENT

Think of at least one villain from your real life. If you're lucky and haven't met a truly nasty or evil person, perhaps you can think of someone whose selfishness or greed or lack of consideration could inspire you. Take notes of their methods, manners, facial expressions, turns of phrase, and choose some elements you can transfer to your fiction villain.

CHAPTER 8: THE VILLAIN'S LAIR

Your novel may feature a scene in the villain's workspace or home. Even if the reader never gets to see the place, this chapter will help you understand your villain's mind better.

The equipment, furnishing and decorations of the villain's lair may reflect some - but probably not all - of the following:

- Tools and machinery for his evil deeds
- Representations of what he values
- Image projectors
- Status symbols
- Surveillance and security
- Intimidation
- Means of communication
- Escape route

TOOLS AND MACHINERY

If the villain operates from his home or workspace, it will be equipped with the tools of his trade. The Obsessed Scientist's laboratory contains cages for animals or humans and everything needed for experiments. The Sadist may have a cell for his captive or a torture chamber adjoining his office, fitted out with manacles and torture machines.

On the other hand, the villain may choose to do his handiwork away from his home or office. The Sadist, for example, may carry out his serial killing in the streets. Some villains (the Evil Overlord, for example) may let others carry out the violence, so their own office looks almost ordinary.

REPRESENTATIONS OF HIS VALUES

What does this villain care about? There will be at least one item reflecting this, and possibly several. The Obsessed Scientist may surround himself with specialist books, charts and graphs, especially those related to his progress and his goal. The Bully may have a picture of a ruthless dictator from history whom he views as a role model, such as Hitler or Stalin, or he may fill the wall with action movie posters or artwork depicting violence. In the home of the Smothering Mother, there'll be the offspring's graduation and wedding photos.

These items may relate to the villain's goal, motivation or compassionate side. They are probably displayed where the villain sees them, perhaps on the wall facing his desk.

IMAGE PROJECTORS

What image does the villain want to project to his staff, visitors and associates? If he wants to be seen as a loyal patriot, there'll be his nation's banner, a portrait of the king, or photos of past presidents. If he wishes to be seen as devoutly religious, there'll be a crucifix, painting or statue of a deity, or other symbol of his religion. Other possibilities are a photo of the villain shaking hands with a famous person with whom he wants to be associated, or a motto or mission statement. These are most likely on the wall behind his desk, where the visitor sees them.

In addition, the villain may display framed newspaper clippings reporting his good deeds, and letters from grateful subjects praising his kindness and generosity.

The villain may also create a space that projects an innocent image. The Sadist who kills victims in the secret torture chamber will mislead investigators with homely items such as baby food, knitting projects and cuddly toys.

STATUS SYMBOLS

Luxury items and status symbols may be selected to impress visitors, or to make the villain himself feel good. If he suffered poverty and deprivation in his childhood, he may indulge in luxuries such as Persian rugs on the floor and original sculptures by famous artists. They may be blatant, or they may be tasteful and subtle.

If he displays status, how does he choose them? Does he simply order the most expensive items in his catalogue, does he send his secretary to buy the best, does he hire an expert consultant, or is he himself a connoisseur?

SURVEILLANCE AND SECURITY

Villains like privacy. Some never allow anyone into their inner sanctum, while others make sure that only invited visitors can get in.

There may be windows overlooking the front gate, sentries outside the estate entrance and the office door, a moat with a drawbridge, tripwires, spy cameras and more. The Evil Overlord especially goes to great lengths to achieve complete control over who may approach. In Fantasy and Science Fiction, he may even have built-in means to destroy unwanted visitors before they reach him.

INTIMIDATION

Some villains aim to make visitors uncomfortable and to impress them with their power. Spatial design can achieve this. For example, the office has much more space behind the desk than in front of it, and the visitor's chair is lower than the villain's, forcing the visitor to look up. This works well for villains who like to terrify and intimidate their staff and associates, especially The Bully, but the more sophisticated and far-sighted villains may do the opposite. They may make their staff and visitors comfortable and delude them into thinking the villain a nice, egalitarian, approachable kind of guy.

MEANS OF COMMUNICATION

Your villain probably has an extensive communication network at his fingertips, and his lair is equipped with state-of-the-art communication technology. There'll be not just one computer but several, as well as landline telephones, mobile phones and more. In a historical setting, there'll be a bell to summon servants, heralds waiting to take their master's message, and a dovecote for receiving messenger pigeons.

ESCAPE ROUTE

Villains know they're at risk, and even if they enjoy the danger, they're prepared for the moment when they're found out. The office has a back door, the castle a subterranean passage, the old house a ladder into the attic which leads into the neighbour's home. The lair also contains a full set of clothes for rapid disguise and a briefcase with fake identity documents. A horse, car, or helicopter may be waiting just outside in readiness at all times. The existence of an escape route depends on the villain's wealth. If he can afford it, he'll have one.

The Evil Overlord may have several escape routes because he is prepared for everything. For the Sadist, the escape route is part of his strategic planning. The Bully, who is often a coward at heart, will make sure he can get out. The Smothering Mother and the Fanatic may not have escape routes because it may not occur to them that they're in danger, while the Social Reject may not care what happens to him.

ASSIGNMENT

Close your eyes and visualise your villain's workspace. If she has no workshop or office, imagine her kitchen, her garden shed or her car, wherever she hangs out a lot. Decide which of the features apply to your villain's lair, and jot down some descriptive notes.

Even if your reader never gets to see this place, this is an eye-opening exercise during which you can learn much about your villain's personality.

CHAPTER 9: HENCHMEN AND MINIONS

Most villains have subordinates or a social network they rely on.

Avoid the cliché of the villain who terrifies people into following him and who kills his lieutenants for the slightest mistake. These methods would work only in the short term because they inspire no loyalty. The unwilling followers would take the first opportunity to side with the hero and depose the villain.

The true villain inspires such loyalty and affection in his followers that they're willing to lay down their lives for him, swear false oaths to give him an alibi and trap the hero.

VILLAINS WITH AND WITHOUT MINIONS

The Evil Overlord always has minions, often a whole horde of them. The Schemer, the Seductress, the Bully and the Smothering Mother usually have at least some.

Other villains have no followers, either because they don't inspire popularity (this is often the case with the Obsessed Scientist and the Social Reject) or because they like to operate in solitude (for example the Sadist).

INNOCENT ALLIES

Sometimes, the villain has staunch supporters in his friends and family. They cannot believe that he is evil. This is especially true of the Sadist. His wife, his neighbours and his priest are convinced that he is a good guy, that he would never harm a woman let alone disembowel dozens, and that the police are hounding him without fair cause.

VASSALS AND EMPLOYEES

If the villain is a king, a politician, a rebel leader or a conquering general, his followers may have an official duty to support him. He controls them absolutely... and they love it. He wins new followers all the time, because he offers wonderful incentives. He gives them castles, titles, money, promotions and anything else they desire so they sign up for his service. Once they're committed, he rewards their loyalty generously... but he also uses threats and punishments.

Small gestures of generosity endear him to his henchmen. Adolf Hitler is a good example. One day, he saw a soldier standing guard in the freezing cold, and gave him his gloves. This was no hardship for Hitler who could obtain another pair of gloves quickly and easily, but to the soldier the Führer's kindness meant the world. With this small gesture - word about which spread fast - Hitler had ensured the loyalty not only of this soldier, but of the soldier's comrades, the soldier's family, and soldiers everywhere in Germany.

Disloyalty, however, gets punished severely, and anyone trying to leave the villain's service will probably not survive.

The blend of carrot and stick is characteristic especially for the villain's rulership style, especially the Evil Overlord, the Smothering Mother and the Bully.

The villain does not trust anyone completely, not even his loyal sidekick. The Evil Overlord in particular spies on and controls his henchmen, and his suspicions may grow into waves of paranoia when he executes his most loyal followers as traitors. Once he has reached this stage, he'll rule by terror which encourages genuine traitors. This is the stage when the hero can defeat him.

ALLIES

The villain may have allies who believe him to be a genuine friend. He goes out of his way to create the impression that he is loyal and supportive. In truth, he has selected these allies for their usefulness, and once their service is no longer needed, or they've become a liability instead of an asset, he'll drop them without qualms.

The Schemer and the Evil Overlord excel at pretending to be friends.

VILLAINOUS MINIONS

Sometimes, a villain's henchmen are other villains. This works well in Historical, Fantasy and Science Fiction. In this case, the villain at the top is almost certainly an Evil Overlord, and the other villains are his lieutenants and vassals.

The Evil Overlord uses his psychological insights to motivate them. He lures and keeps each by giving them what they want. The Obsessed Scientist is happy to find an employer who funds his expensive cancer research, the Smothering Mother is grateful that the Evil Overlord pays her son's college fees, the Fanatic values the support for his crusade, and the Bully rejoices in a job where he gets paid to intimidate victims.

If you have several connected villains in your story, identify who is the most dangerous one. This is probably - though not always - the Evil Overlord at the top of the power pyramid. Your hero needs to defeat the minor villains first, keeping the big villain for the final confrontation at the novel's climax.

THE EVIL OVERLORD'S ORGANISATION

Some villains have a whole staff of minions and an extensive network of supporters. The Evil Overlord in particular may categorise his followers in four groups depending on their trustworthiness.

Group 1: The Trusted Lieutenants

These are the Evil Overlord's inner circle, the ones on whom he can rely absolutely. He has few secrets from them and delegates difficult and sensitive tasks to them. They are aware of his ruthlessness and brutality, and they support it. They are usually motivated by the cause of which the Evil Overlord is the leader and figurehead. They may also be motivated by ambition. You can create exciting plot twists when one of the lieutenants betrays the Evil Overlord, or when he gets paranoid with suspicion and executes his faithful lieutenants.

Group 2: The Competent Supporters

These people share his ideals, values and goal. They support him wholeheartedly and are willing to accept his sometimes unsavoury methods. Whenever something important but not top-secret needs to be done, he'll get someone from this group to carry it out. He also uses them for dangerous or dirty work, because they are expendable. When the police or the press find out about the dirty deed, he'll claim it was carried out without his knowledge, pretend outrage and fire the person who was in charge.

He motivates them with generous rewards for good service. He offers better pay and more benefits than any other employer, and provides childcare and pension schemes. With startling generosity, he finances their college education, pays for specialist treatment for their sick child, finds their missing nephew or gets their brother's prison sentence overturned. Their financial dependence on him and their gratitude for his help make them loyal and willing to do almost anything for him.

Group 3: The Clueless Groupies

These naive people are easily led or misled. They think he's nice guy or a noble hero, believe his public image and his propaganda, and treat any hint of the truth as a malicious rumour.

He needs them to maintain his image, but does not trust them one bit. They may include family, neighbours, church congregation, fans, and some members of his staff.

Group 4: The Unwilling Vassals

Not everyone chooses to work for the Evil Overlord. Some do it under duress or out of fear. The people of conquered nations resent his rule.

The biologist helps him develop a devastating biological weapon because if she refuses, the Evil Overlord will slaughter her children.

He doesn't motivate these people but coerces them with threats. They obey his demands because they fear the consequences of displeasing him. They fear the consequences of disobeying or displeasing him, so they do what he wants.

They are not loyal. At the first chance to defect safely, they will defect. Naturally, the Evil Overlord knows they are not trustworthy, does not let them into any secrets, and makes sure they don't get the opportunity to betray him or defect. In your story, some unwilling vassals will take the risk and side with the hero. When the Evil Overlord catches them, he punishes them cruelly to set an example.

Other Villains in the Evil Overlord's Employ

The Evil Overlord likes to recruit other villains to do his dirty work. They belong to the first and second group. He knows what makes each of them tick, and manipulates them.

The Bully is perfect for intimidation jobs and for roughing people up, and he'll enjoy the assignments the Evil Overlord sends him on.

The Smothering Mother works for him because of his patronage of her family. He pays her sons' college fees, finds titled husbands for her daughters and gets her favourite brother out of jail. In return, she does anything he wants, such as destroying evidence and providing a false alibi.

The Obsessed Scientist, grateful that the Evil Overlord values his expertise and funds his research, develops the weapons of mass destruction his employer wants.

The Fanatic is grateful for the generous donations to the sacred cause, and willing to slaughter the people the Evil Overlord points out as blasphemous infidels.

ASSIGNMENT

Tell us about your villain's supporters. How does he keep them motivated, loyal and under control?

CHAPTER 10: THE FINAL SHOWDOWN

Almost every novel has a climax near the end of the book. This is when all the plot strands come together and the heroine (or hero) faces her greatest challenge. The tension is so high that the reader perches on the edge of her seat, unable to tear herself away from the story's action.

Try to plot your story so your hero and your villain meet in a final showdown. In some books (especially thrillers), the confrontation between hero and villain is the core of the climax. In others, the showdown serves to add tension and excitement to other plot elements. For example, in a romance, the hero and the heroine fight side by side against the villain and his minions. They realise that they're meant to be together, and plan to marry - if they survive this terrible danger.

Here are tips how to give your readers an unforgettable climax with the hero versus villain confrontation.

- Don't rush the climax. The reader has been waiting for this. Spread it out over a whole scene or even several, especially in a thriller.
- The hero and the villain are not equally matched. Stack the advantages in the villain's favour. The villain is prepared, knows the terrain and has better weapons while the hero is injured, exhausted and unarmed.
- Raise the stakes. During this final showdown, a lot is at stake, for example the hero's survival, the lives of loved ones, the existence of an endangered species, the future of the planet, or world peace. If the villain wins, he will attain his goal, and the hero (and maybe the whole village or the whole world) will perish.
- Increase the excitement by adding an element of danger. Does your hero have a phobia? Perhaps he is scared of fire, of heights

or of snakes. Whatever frightens him, if he has successfully avoided it during the novel, during the climax he must confront his fears. The only way to survive and to rescue her loved ones is to enter the burning building, to scale the cliff or to jump into the snake pit.

Perhaps you can plot it so your devious villain knows of the phobia and has arranged the snake pit.

- Choose an unusual location, perhaps one which is weird or dangerous - or both. How about a derelict rollercoaster, the rainforest canopy, a sinking cruise ship, a cable car dangling above an abyss, a dam about to burst, or an abandoned mineshaft? If possible, make it a place the villain is familiar with and the hero is not. It may even be the villain's lair.

ASSIGNMENT

If you have already planned or drafted the final showdown/climax scene, consider if you could move it to a more exciting location, raise the stakes, add more danger, or stake the odds more in the villain's favour.

If you haven't started the scene yet, jot down some ideas. You can always change these later.

CHAPTER 11: DIALOGUE AND TONE OF VOICE

When your villain talks, make her dialogue short and to the point. The tighter her speech, the more intelligent and threatening it becomes. Wordy waffling would dilute the effect, so prune your villain's dialogue. The fewer words she uses, the more impact they have. Her henchmen and victims may babble, but not she.

Consider giving your villain a catchphrase, some kind of comment she uses in different situations. This can be chilling.

To give your reader a sense of foreboding, a creepy feeling or a distinct chill, describe what the villain's voice sounds like. Is it high-pitched or deep, resonant or raspy?

Similes (comparing the voice to another sound) work well, especially if the comparison is something dangerous from the point-of-view character's range of experience. Does it remind the PoV of wind howling in a chimney, grinding metal, a strict teacher, a hypnotist, an Alsatian's growl or an un-oiled hinge?

You can use these phrases:

His voice sounded like ...

His voice reminded her of ...

Her voice had the ... of a ...

He spoke in the tone of a ...

Her voice held a note of ...

... swung in her voice.

... his voice laden with ...

Here are examples from my own fiction, describing dangerous characters. Please don't copy these sentences, but you may find them inspiring for your own ideas.

Kirral's voice had the soft scraping tone of a sword grinding against a whetstone. (Storm Dancer)

His voice had the low-humming hiss of a wasp hovering over rotting fruit. (Storm Dancer)

Baryush spoke with the sonorous tone of a satisfied customer. (Storm Dancer)

His voice softened to the texture of rubber. (Storm Dancer)

He intoned an invocation of the Red Goddess, his voice deep and resonant like that of the solo baritone in Kathy's church choir. (Druid Stones)

His voice had a sharp edge. (Druid Stones)

...he assured her, using the same tone as a dentist telling a patient it would hurt just a little. (Druid Stones)

... he says in his soft singsong voice. (Beltane)

His voice is deep and brisk. (Beltane)

Dirk's voice was heavy with importance, reminding us that underlings must follow their leader. (I Dived the Pandora)

Dirk lectured in his preacher's voice. (I Dived The Pandora)

Her voice whined like a dentist's drill, shrill, painful, persistent. (Seagulls)

You can use this technique several times in your novel, as long as you use different descriptions. Perhaps during the villain's first appearance, the voice doesn't sound all that bad, but the simile may hint at something not entirely good. This plants a sense of danger in the reader's subconscious without giving anything away. Once the villain's true nature is revealed, the voice descriptions can be explicitly dangerous.

When you include a sentence about the sound of the voice, you don't need 'he/she said' because that's implied.

ASSIGNMENT

Write one line of dialogue for your villain. Make it short, pithy, to the point. It may be your villain's catchphrase. Follow this with a sentence describing the sound of the villain's voice.

CHAPTER 12: HANDS AND CLAWS

To increase suspense in a scene where the villain is about to do something nasty, slow down the pace and describe his hands. This is perfect for when the Evil Overlord signs the order to exterminate the children, or when the torturer readies his instruments.

Are the hands bronzed or pale, wrinkled or smooth? Are the fingers long or stubby, bony or pudgy?

Describe the colour and texture of the skin. Wrinkled, calloused or smooth? Show the way the hands move. Perhaps you can use a simile, comparing them to something else - fingers like spider's legs, precision movements like a surgeon's - but only if it suits the story.

Spend a moment on the nails. Are they prawn-pink or nicotine-yellow? Splintered, dirty, or perfectly manicured? Is the varnish chipped, or does it display the latest fashion in nail art?

In many people's subconscious, long fingernails create unease, so consider giving your dangerous character longer than average nails. However, male villains with very long nails are a cliché of horror flicks, so don't overdo it.

Use the same technique if the villain is a dangerous animal or fantasy monster. Describe the front paws, their texture, colour, shape and movement. Are they webbed, scaled, furry or naked? Focus on the claws: straight like rapiers or curved like scimitars? Translucent like white glass, or black like glistening obsidian?

Even more chilling is the experience of being touched by those hands. Do they feel cold, warm, icy or hot? Dry or damp? Rough or smooth? Soft or hard?

Here are some examples from my published fiction. Please don't copy them, but they may serve as inspiration for your own ideas.

> *His fingers glinted with rings.* (Storm Dancer)
>
> *His calloused fingers brush my neck.* (Beltane)
>
> *... and patted my wrist with flabby fingers.* (I Dived the Pandora)
>
> *His big hand gripped my arm.* (Through the Tunnel)
>
> *The ghost clamped an icy hand around Jean's arm.* (Take me to St Roch's)
>
> *In close-up reality, they were ugly, unromantic beasts, from the wrinkled flat clawed feet and the grey-pink legs to the folded wings ending in feathers like black blades.* (Seagulls)
>
> *Four bony hands clawed into Estelle's flesh.* (Four Bony Hands)
>
> *She took the clay beaker from his manicured fingers and sipped.* (Druid Stones)
>
> *The chief druid's hands clasped her arms like iron grips.* (Druid Stones)
>
> *His hard hand pulled me away from the table.* (Burning)

A single sentence about the evil person's hands can increase the sense of danger or evil greatly. However, you must choose the right place to insert it, ideally when the hands are about to do something cruel. The point-of-view character must be able to see (or feel) them.

ASSIGNMENT

Write a sentence about something the villain does with his hands, describing how the hands look, feel or move.

CHAPTER 13: SCARY SMILES

An evil villain's smile can send chills sliding down the reader's spine. Make the most of it. Don't just write 'he smiled' or 'he smiled slowly/knowingly/cruelly.'

Instead, devote a full sentence to describing this smile. Here are some ideas to get you started. If you want to use them, I recommend you rewrite them in your own words so they suit your story, your villain, and your personal writing style.

> *Her eyes lit, and her lips curved in malicious pleasure.*
>
> *The corners of her mouth turned up.*
>
> *His smile bared large, glistening teeth.*
>
> *His upper lip curled with mirth.*
>
> *Her face slid into an insincere smile.*
>
> *His mouth curved like a scimitar.*
>
> *Although her mouth curved, the smile did not reach her eyes.*

Here are examples of how I've used smiles for unpleasant and dangerous people in my own fiction. Please don't copy these, but view them as inspiration to create something that's unique to your story:

> *Lord Govan put on his official smile to receive the leather-wrapped parcel.* (Storm Dancer)
>
> *The Consort's smile spread the ends of his moustache.* (Storm Dancer)

> *His mouth spread into a smile so wide that the moustache quivered.* (Storm Dancer)
>
> *Her smile was soft, her gaze hard.* (Storm Dancer)
>
> *Kirral's smile was knife-edge thin.* (Storm Dancer)
>
> *Baryush's smile bared large teeth.* (Storm Dancer)
>
> *There was a contorted smile on her face, as if she wanted to reassure me that she still loved me.* (Never Leave Me)
>
> *The guide inclined her head, granting the child what was almost a smile.* (The Painted Staircase)
>
> *The pinched face softened at last, and her mouth curved into a smile.* (The Painted Staircase)

Use this technique sparingly. Novice writers tend to overuse smiles; their heroes, heroines, villains and supporting cast smile all the time, and this soon becomes tedious.

The fewer smiles you use, the better, especially for the dangerous characters.

The villain's smile has the greatest impact if he smiles only this once. In a long novel, he may smile several times... but not on every page. If he smiles all the time, the effect wears off. The rarer the smile, the greater the chill effect.

ASSIGNMENT

Write a sentence describing your villain's smile. Keep it simple.

CHAPTER 14: HEROES AND VILLAINS - SOME DEFINITIONS

These definitions aren't clear cut. They overlap and are sometimes used interchangeably.

Protagonist

This is the main character of the story, the one who sets out to achieve a goal and makes things happen. Usually, the protagonist, the hero and the point of view are the same person.

Antagonist

This character stands in the way of the hero's goal. Often - but not always - this is a villain. It could also be a good guy who is a rival for the love of the same woman, or for the job the hero wants.

Hero

This is the 'good' person in the story. In most works of fiction, the hero is the protagonist.

In romance novels, the word 'hero' refers to the female protagonist's male love interest.

Heroine

This term is used either as the female form of 'hero' or for the male protagonist's female love interest.

Point of View (PoV)

The PoV is the character through whom the reader experiences the story. This is usually, but not always, the protagonist.

Villain PoV may not work well for a novel, because readers don't enjoy being inside the evil person for such a long time. However, it can make great short stories, especially in the horror genre.

Some novels have the same PoV for the whole book. Others use different PoVs for different sections, for example, the hero's PoV for one chapter, the villain's for the next, then the victim's and then the hero's again.

Not all novels have a PoV character. Some, especially 19th century classics, use a godlike perspective where the reader can see into every character's mind.

Flawed Hero

This is a hero who is not all pure and good, but has a weakness or character flaw. Flawed heroes can be more interesting and real than flawless ones. The flawed hero usually grows during the story and learns to overcome his weakness.

Dark Hero

This person is similar to the flawed hero, and the terms are sometimes used interchangeably. However, the dark hero is more seriously flawed, and poses a danger to others. This character may even be a hero and a villain at the same time.

Dark hero stories often probe the boundaries between good and evil and have psychological depth. They can create strong emotions in the readers.

The Dark hero works well in paranormal romance, urban fantasy and westerns. Of the villain archetypes, the Social Reject - smouldering, tortured, bitter, lonely and brave - is most suitable.

Anti-Hero

This term is sometimes used interchangeably with 'flawed hero' and 'dark hero', or for 'badass hero with lousy manners'. However, its main meaning is a protagonist who doesn't have the usual attributes of a hero. He lacks drive and courage, and instead of setting out to achieve a goal and making things happen, the anti-hero stumbles passively through life and things happen to him.

He is like most people in real life. This makes it easy for the reader to identify with him. However, the anti-hero doesn't provide the exciting escapism most readers enjoy in a story. Passive anti-heroes rarely work in genre fiction, but they can be perfect for literary fiction and comedies.

Villain

The villain is an evil person and usually the antagonist. This whole book is about villains.

Take note of the spelling: 'villain' not 'villian'. The word is derived from Middle English, medieval French and Latin.

Villainess

This word is sometimes used to denote a female villain.

Psychopath

Sometimes used interchangeably with 'sociopath'. Both have antisocial personality disorders.

The main difference is that the psychopath is not entirely sane. She is not fully in touch with reality, may have delusions or hallucinations, or suffer from extreme obsessions, and may not understand the difference between right and wrong. A psychopath may be sent to an institution for the criminally insane instead of to a normal prison, or may be found 'not guilty by reason of insanity' and sent to a psychiatric facility for treatment.

Sociopath

Unlike the psychopath, the sociopath is sane. He knows the difference between right and wrong but chooses to ignore it. His absence of empathy with others and his lack of conscience make him the scariest of villains. Since he is sane, he'll act normal most of the time, and may be a model father and pillar of the community - but he is a ruthless predator.

The typical sociopath has a huge ego and cares only about himself, although he may pretend to care for other people. He is a habitual liar and has no qualms about taking advantage of others.

In real life, a large number of ruthless criminals and cruel despots are sociopaths. In fiction, the sociopath's profile best fits the Evil Overlord and the Sadist. If you're writing serial killer thrillers, your villain is probably a sociopath.

Sanity is relative, and these brief explanations are not clinical definitions. For a more thorough analysis, you may want to read up on anti-social disorders.

ASSIGNMENT

Which, if any, of these definitions apply to the characters in your story?

CHAPTER 15: CLICHES TO AVOID

Some characteristics and plot devices have been used so often they've become clichés. Instead of grabbing the reader's imagination, they elicit boredom or snorts.

Here's a list. Avoid them unless your story needs them.

1. Evil Laughter

In the early and mid-twentieth century, radio plays and movies commonly featured a villain with maniacal laughter. Actors specialising in villain roles refined their maniacal laughter skills, radio stations had pre-recorded evil laughs to insert into plays and writers sprinkled their fiction with maniacal '*Mwahahaha!*' '*Bwuhuhuhaha muwhahaha!*' This became such a stock tool, especially in fantasy, that listeners, viewers and readers came to regard it as a joke.

Avoid the evil laughter if you want your readers to take your villain seriously. A cruel smile is often more effective.

If your story requires evil laughter, use it, but instead of *Mwahahaha* and *Bruhuwaha* describe the sound, for example:

> *His laughter echoed through the cave, roaring and deep.*

2. Ugliness

The Victorians believed that good and evil showed on a person's face, and that you only needed a quick glance to tell if a person was trustworthy. A handsome face indicated honesty, while ugliness was a sure indicator of evil. Unsurprisingly, the good guys of Victorian fiction were always pleasant to look at, while the bad guys could be recognised by their facial deformities.

Modern readers reject such prejudices. They know that few people have the facial features they deserve, and may find such stereotyping offensive.

A handsome villain offers far greater scope for fiction, because he can get away with more. Although few people today are as prejudiced towards handsomeness as the Victorians were, they still tend to trust a good-looking person more.

If your villain possesses attractive looks, he can more convincingly pose as a hospital doctor or swindle victims out of their life savings. The pretty young woman with innocent blue eyes can more easily persuade the ageing millionaire to name her his heiress than her ugly sister could, and the beautiful seductress with the perfect body will have more success at leading men into sin than a plain girl.

The villains of the Confidence Trickster and Seductress archetypes are probably very good-looking.

This does not mean that every villain in every story needs to be beautiful. Your villain's ugliness may have helped shape his attitudes. If you've chosen the Social Reject archetype, he may have been shunned by society from an early age because of a large birthmark on his face, or perhaps an accident or illness left him disfigured. He feels bitter and resentful about being ugly.

3. Hot Stinking Breath

This has been overused especially in the historical and romance genres. Whenever a villain or villainous henchman tries to force a kiss on the heroine or to rip her bodice, he seems to have hot stinking breath.

If you want to use it, make it less obviously clichéd by phrasing it differently. Instead of using the words hot stinking breath, describe the smell.

Her breath stank of beer and nicotine.

His breath reeked of vomit and decayed teeth.

4. Punishing Minions for Failure

Pulp novels, comics and B movies often show the Evil Overlord cruelly punishing minions for failure. Whenever an employee reports that he has failed at a task, the Evil Overlord snaps his fingers and orders whipping or execution. This is predictable as well as implausible.

Minions who fear punishment won't go out of their way to serve the great man. Instead, they'll seek the first opportunity to defect. The Evil Overlord is not that stupid. Rather, he rewards minions generously for good service, and if someone fails in a mission, he sends them for retraining.

However, he punishes betrayal. Anyone who dares to deceive him or to defect will be punished brutally. He has no mercy or forgiveness for disloyalty, and a mere suspicion of treachery is enough to unleash his wrath. The bodies of the traitors he crucified rot outside the castle walls, a feast for the crows and a deterrent for others.

5. Stupidity

Many writers make their villains stupid, to show the hero's cleverness - but that makes the villain forgettable and the story dull.

Intelligent villains are much more interesting and pose a genuine challenge for the hero.

6. Total Evil

Villains who are evil to everyone on every occasion in every way are predictable and boring, cardboard characters whom the reader soon forgets. The villains who stick in the reader's mind are the ones whose attitude and behaviour vary with the situation.

The best villains are ruthless and cruel to some people, but exceedingly pleasant and kind to others.

The archetype may give you a clue:

- *The Smothering Mother* is evil only to those who get in the way of her vision for her family.

- *The Evil Overlord* is cruel to those who have betrayed him and ruthless to those who oppose him, but otherwise he is helpful and supportive.

- *The Sadist* is evil only to his carefully selected victim group. The rest of the world knows him as a really nice guy.

- *The Social Reject* hurts only those he believes have harmed him.

- *The Confidence Trickster* harms others only if there's a financial gain in it for him.

- *The Schemer and the Seductress* don't seek to hurt others, although they don't seek to avoid it either.

- *The Fanatic* is evil only to the infidels who oppose his fanaticism or don't share his beliefs.

- *The Bully* is evil only to those who are weaker than him. He doesn't have the courage to oppose those with more power.

7. Leaves the Captured Hero to Die

The villain finally has the hero in his power, and punishes him with a slow, gruesome death - but he doesn't stay around. Instead, he goes off somewhere else and leaves the hero to his peril. Of course, the resourceful hero finds a way to escape. This is such a common plot device in movies and books that it may make your readers groan.

It also stretches credulity. The intelligent villain - especially the Evil Overlord - wouldn't take such a risk. He wouldn't leave until he's sure that the hero is really dead, and then he'd shoot the corpse in the head, just to make sure. The Obsessed Scientist would not take any risks either. The Social Reject who has waited all his life for this moment will not miss the chance to savour his revenge. The Bully and The Sadist would also hang around to enjoy every moment of the hero's suffering and fear.

If you want the villain to absent himself in this crucial moment, you need to give him a compelling reason to take the risk and miss the fun.

ASSIGNMENT

Does your story draft contain any of these clichés? If yes, could you get rid of it or make it less obvious?

CHAPTER 16: MEET KIRRAL, THE VILLAIN OF STORM DANCER

Many readers have emailed me to say how much they love Kirral... from a distance. Of all my characters, Kirral is probably the most popular. He gets more fan mail then my heroes.

Kirral is the Obsessed Scientist archetype. In creating him and writing about him, I employed most of the techniques from this book.

Here are several excerpts, showing Kirral from different points of view. If you like, try to spot which techniques I have applied where.

To avoid plot spoilers, I've not included Kirral's most interesting cruelties.

From Chapter 1, Scene 2, Dahoud's Point of View

At the entrance to the royal audience hall, green-uniformed guards confiscated Dahoud's dagger-belt. The door thudded shut behind him.

Light seeped through slitted windows, painting stripes on the carpet. Rows of whitewood benches stood empty, as if waiting for spectators to stream in and take their seats. The Consort Kirral sat on an elevated divan, a jewel-encrusted white turban on his head, his moustache shaped into a pair of pointed blades. The steep platform bearing the divan forced visitors to gaze upwards, a technique Dahoud himself had often used to intimidate callers.

"Highness, you summoned me."

Grape-green eyes peered from under dark bushy brows. Kirral cracked a saltnut between his teeth and spat the empty shell on the carpet at Dahoud's feet. Dahoud permitted himself no response. Standing as straight as a soldier before his commanding officer, he inhaled deeply of the stale incense and old breath that lay in the air, and waited.

A mural of the Queen, a white full-moon face under an ornamental headdress, dominated the room, reminding audience-seekers that she was the true ruler of Quislak – even if she took little interest in politics. She left the day-to-day government to her Consort, who in turn delegated most work to his head-wife.

"Would you like some saltnuts, young man?" Kirral's voice had the soft scraping tone of a sword grinding against a whetstone.

To take the nuts from the Consort's outstretched hand, Dahoud had to walk up to the platform and look up, the way a lapdog accepted morsels. Kirral grinned, and his slippered feet wiggled in anticipation.

If the Consort gained pleasure from humiliating visitors, pride was a waste of time. "Thank you, Highness."

"The Koskarans ransack our settlements, rob our caravans, slaughter our people." Kirral twisted a saltnut between his fingers, as if assessing its value. "Are you the man who subdued those savages four years ago?"

"I am." Dahoud glanced at the statues lining the cedar-panelled walls. He had looted many of those marble deities from temples in conquered lands, including Koskara. Now they queued at floor level, paying homage to Quislak's nine Mighty Ones, who stood haughtily on a brocaded dais. "If my experience may be of use, I'll gladly advise the general in charge."

Kirral cracked another nut. "I want you to squash those rebels to pulp."

"You need a different man, Highness."

"I need the Black Besieger, and I will get him." Kirral stroked the parchment scrolls at his side with a lover's caress. "My favourite reading matter: personal dossiers. These are from your employers, past and present. You were the youngest general in the Queendom's history, the first ethnic Samili to rise to that rank. Then you threw your career into the dust." Kirral's eyes focused like a hawk's before the kill. "Why?"

"Personal reasons."

"Your personal reasons entertain me," Kirral said. "During a fine game of Siege last night, I asked my good friend Paniour why the Black Besieger quit. I learnt that he had a sudden attack of conscience. Not about battlefield deaths, but the treatment of captives."

Dahoud stayed silent.

"To fool the world that the Black Besieger no longer existed, you spread rumours about his death. His supposed demise occurred not on the battlefield, but at the hands of an enraged woman. How imaginative." Kirral cackled like a spotted hyena. "Paniour tells me you imagined yourself possessed by a djinn. A mythical creature from nomad lore."

Dahoud knew better than to insist on the gruesome truth of demonic possession. "It was a figure of speech."

Kirral's bushy brows rose to his turban rim and stayed there. "For two years, all traces of you vanished as if you had indeed died. What did you do before Govan took you on?"

"Labour." The kind of work a Samili could get: digging latrines, dragging a builder's brick-loads like a sweating donkey, stirring a dyer's pots of boiling piss.

"Watching you would have been educational. A leopard may dress as a rabbit, but he will find the garments too small."

Dahoud said nothing.

"Last year, one of Satrap Govan's regular reports held an interesting paragraph. When the earthquake struck, a minor clerk led the rescue efforts 'with courage and quick thought, and with the efficiency of a general'. The clerk was an ethnic Samili with a sketchy history. Naturally, this clerk interested me. Alas." Kirral leant back into the divan, and the corners of his mouth twitched as if something amused him. "Govan's opinion changed. Now he rants about your lack of manners, your insolence, the ideas you have above your station, how he wants to kick you out of office and send you to count goat-droppings in the Samil." Kirral's voice lowered to a confidential whisper. "Tell me, young man: Are you courting your employer's daughter?"

Dahoud's face fired. Esha's white dimpled cheeks and soft voice had captured him. Whenever they met at work, she granted him a friendly word, and twice he had escorted her to a fantasia show. For the first time in his life, a woman seemed to like him.

"A Ladysdaughter has dynastic obligations," Kirral said softly. "Her offspring will only be Ladysdaughters if fathered by a satrap. If the girl has sense, she will not waste herself on a mere clerk." He popped another nut into his mouth.

"Of course." Esha would marry a satrap, or at least, a chief councillor with promotion prospects.

The moustache blades quivered with every chewing motion. "Two days ago, more news came from Koskara. This is not public knowledge yet. Satrap Zetan is dead, apparently poisoned by rebels. His councillors barricaded themselves into the residency. What do you think of their decision?"

"They're brave." They were foolish. Dahoud remembered the residency: a greenstone palace with pillars and pilasters, fancy and fragile, not designed to withstand a siege. "Are women among them?"

Kirral's lips curved as if the question gave him malicious pleasure. "Would it make a difference to you if there were? If the Black Besieger squashes those rebels, I will make him the new lord-satrap of Koskara."

Dahoud stood very still. Lord-satrap? He checked the Consort's posture: leaning forward, hands tented, lips pursed, eyes intent.

"Think about it, Dahoud. No more labouring, no more clerking, no more grovelling before Govan. More power than you ever had as a general. Your own satrapy to shape into an oasis of peace where you can keep the womenfolk safe." The Consort's smile spread the ends of his moustache. "And I shall send Esha Ladysdaughter as your bride."

Power, respect, peace, a woman who liked him, all served on a silver platter – if he unsheathed his sword again, if he devastated Koskara once more, if he besieged the rebels' strongholds. During a siege, anger and lust built a pyre on which the noblest resolutions burnt to ashes. He might again become the monster he had fought so hard to leave behind.

"What if I decline?"

Kirral beamed as if Dahoud's reaction had lit pleasure lanterns behind his eyes. "Then you will stay here at the palace. I will give you a job suiting your particular talents and interests: torturer in charge of females. You will enjoy that. The choice is yours."

Dahoud's blood chilled. "I'll go to Koskara."

"Good choice, Dahoud. The high general Paniour awaits you."

On his way out, Dahoud sent silent a prayer to the Great Mare, the horse-headed woman who protected Koskara.

From Chapter 3, Scene 3, Merida's Point of View

The crowd parted, letting Merida pass. She felt their tense gazes in her back as she strode down the unlit corridor. The clacking of her boots sent tiny lizards darting for cover.

Her knock on the red door yielded no reply. When she pushed, the door whined inwards on its hinges. The temperature dropped. The cool air was thick with incense.

A man reposed cross-legged on a divan. On his head squatted a pumpkin-coloured turban like a fat hen on an egg, revealing little of his face beyond a knife-shaped moustache. Pale legs stuck out of a short tunic and ended in pink pointy slippers with big pompoms. Bent over a Siege gaming board, he did not acknowledge her arrival.

Quietly, she let the door click into its frame and spoke her rehearsed introduction in fluent Quislaki. "I am Merida, second daughter of the First Family of Karr of Hohenhegen, personal value of 248, eleventh-degree magician, special ambassador for the Virtuous Republic of Riverland."

She waited for him to confirm his identity, but he did not glance up. After counting sixteen heartbeats, she assembled the words for her complaint. "I must inform you of a communication difficulty. Members of your staff seem to assume that I'll sleep in a dormitory."

Still not looking up, he twisted a yellow gaming stone and clacked it into a new position.

For a further thirty-two heartbeats, Merida took in the flower-patterned chipped tiles on the walls, the mural of the map of the Queendom, the shelves untidily crammed with scrolls, the lavishly embroidered but badly stained upholstery of the divans. Then she had enough. She pushed her fists into her waist. "Am I addressing His Highness Lord Kirral, Consort to the High Queen of Quislak?"

He tilted his head at her, balancing a green gaming stone on the tip of his pinkie. "Do you play Siege?"

Could this buffoon be the Consort who ruled the nation on behalf of the Queen? Perhaps she had mistaken the door, or the woman in the corridor had played a practical joke on her. Yet an underling would not dare to play Siege against himself during work hours.

"I possess some trifling skill," she replied stiffly. "But I'm not here to play games. If you want rain for your country, you must honour the terms of the agreement. I cannot and will not work magic unless the conditions are right, including privacy for the preparations. This contract promises a private apartment." She waved the parchment at him.

"I am a busy man." His voice had the low-humming hiss of a wasp hovering over rotting fruit. "I do not have time to keep promises."

He clacked the green token down and pushed the other stones rapidly across the gaming board. His aura pulsed with blue hues of intellectual power so strong it made her skin prickle. He appeared to have forgotten her presence.

Merida stepped forward. "Are you, or aren't you, the Consort Kirral?" she demanded. "Do you, or don't you, want rain for your land?"

At last, he raised his face. His eyes flashed at her, green as polished peridots with jewel-hard brightness. His mouth spread into a smile so wide that the moustache quivered. Merida's skin crawled as if slugs were slithering up her spine.

"Yes, I am the Consort." His voice softened to the texture of rubber. "I look forward to playing with you."

A chill crept across her skin, but the furnace of her anger blasted it away. She would have yelled, were such display of unbridled emotion not un-Riverian. Now that she had a personal value of 248, she would always act with dignity. She dipped a curt bow and marched out, letting the door snap shut behind her.

From Chapter 6, Scene 2, Merida's Point of View

The next fool begged forgiveness for poisoning his neighbour's well.

"Cut off his arm," Kirral said. "Now."

"No! Please, have mercy!" The man tried to run, but two greenbelts restrained him.

Kirral sent the master of the ceremonies back into the arena to announce: "The Consort offers you mercy. He lets you choose: either one arm, or both hands."

A moment later, the well poisoner's scream shuddered through the arena. Merida tried not to look at his crumpled body on the grass, or the arm on the bloodied block, or executioner holding his dripping sword high as in triumph.

From Chapter 23, Scene 4, Merida's Point of View

Then drums rolled for the performance Kirral had requested, an escapologist who claimed the ability to free himself from any fetters. People clustered around the wooden cage. On one side of the partition, the actor was roped to the wooden bars, on the other waited a growling leopard. The sand clock spouted a stream of silver sand into the bowl. Once it was spent, a spectator would pull up the partition, freeing the beast to maul the man. The performer succeeded in undoing the knots and fleeing the cage just as the last grains of sand trickled from the spout.

Kirral congratulated him warmly. "An excellent performance, most educational. I wonder if you would care to repeat it." He rubbed his hands. "If you escape a second time, I will treble your fee. Bear in mind, however, that I have observed closely how you undid those knots. This time, I will tie them so you cannot undo them by the same method. Will you take the risk?"

Merida guessed that if the performer survived, Kirral would tempt him with higher rewards into further and further repeats, each with a higher risk of failure.

From Chapter 27, Scene 1, Tarkan's Point of View

"Highness." Tarkan kept his voice patient and tried not to drum his foot on the carpet. "You were going to brief me about the political plans for Tajlit."

"Tajlit, Tajlit, Tajlit. Every day you pester me about Tajlit." Kirral glowered through the cloud of incense smoke. "Don't I have more important matters to think about? Look at this. Look at it!" He adjusted the tower of quivering greenstone disks on the table before him.

Tarkan chose his comment with care. "This is very high, and it balances beautifully. What does it signify?"

"Research." Kirral steadied the construction with his fingers to stop a tremble, and scrutinised it with his turbaned head tilted and his eyes narrowed to slits. Today, the henna-tinted moustache hovered horizontally. Beads strung along its lower edge gave it the semblance of a serrated knife. "Last night, I permitted thirty men to choose: They could have their large toe nail pulled out without anaesthetic, or be drowsy with poppy juice while their toe was amputated. All thirty opted for the nail." He ran a caressing fingertip down the stacked tokens. "This morning, after they witnessed the torturer do his job on the first man, all the others offered to give their toes in return for the poppy juice. What made them change their minds? The blood, or the screaming, or something else entirely?"

"Perhaps a combination of factors." Tarkan glanced at the scrolls in the spider-webbed shelf, and the desk overspilling with documents and dust. The Consort had not touched real work for some time. "We will never know."

"I must know." Kirral slammed his palm on the table. The token tower trembled and broke. "The sample was too small. Thirty prisoners can't reveal what the average Queendom subject wants. I will repeat the research with a larger segment of the population. A randomly selected village should give a good cross-section of age, gender and occupation. What do you say?"

"Possibly." Tarkan's throat tightened, but he tried once more. "Tajlit has been without a satrap for two moons."

"I told you, Tarkan." Kirral's voice was swift and sharp like the crack of the whip. "Do not bother me with politics."

"Allow me to assume the burden of politics for Tajlit, to free more of your time for vital research."

"You have my permission to depart Tajlit. Go, go, go!"

Tarkan let out a breath he had not known he was holding.

He had reached the door when Kirral called him back. "No, wait! You cannot leave yet. Tomorrow is Fool's Plea!"

"Yes, Highness." Tarkan's throat was constricting again.

"A satrap needs wisdom, and Fool's Plea is the best time to learn. A few fools will win wonderful rewards, while most get punished severely. For the merest chance of a prize, they will endure public humiliation, risking their reputations and their lives." Kirral's purple-slippered feet bounced with excitement. "Watch the fun, witness the pleas, grow wise."

"I will, Highness." Tarkan bowed once more. "Thank you for the opportunity to learn from you."

The Consort's madness was increasing by the hour. Tarkan pitied the people who were staking their lives tomorrow.

From Chapter 27, Scene 3, Dahoud's Point of View

The master of ceremonies, imposing in a green tunic and a large staff with ribbons and bells, introduced his case. "Applause, please, for Amad the weaver and his good-speaker."

Feet stomped and tongues trilled.

"My friend is a loyal subject of the Queen," the good-speaker began with his arms raised as if in prayer, "a lifelong citizen of Quislabat, an honourable practitioner of his trade. Members of the royal guard frequently borrow items from his home – most recently a pair of fine sandals – and refuse to give them back."

Bending forward, Kirral instructed a greenbelt to deliver his judgement.

"Since Amad mourns the loss of his sandals," the greenbelt's voice droned, "It is the Royal Consort's will that he shall never want for sandals again. Cut off his feet." He paused for a roar of approval from the blood-drunk spectators. "Also cut off one leg. Either from Amad, or from his good-speaker. Amad, the choice is yours."

During the screeches of panic and pain, Dahoud stared at his own black-sandalled feet.

The master of ceremonies shook his beribboned staff. "Next, we have, for the first time ever in the history of Fool's Plea Celebrations, a satrap! Please welcome Lord Dahoud, the satrap of Koskara!"

Five thousand voices, drunk with blood-lust, cheered. Ten thousand feet stamped. Dahoud strode into the arena with large, steady steps, waving his arms to display the purple fringe on his wrists. Cold sweat glued the tunic to his skin. Had Kirral already decided the outcome and devised a penalty?

On the blood-soaked patch of grass before the royal grandstand, Tarkan slapped him on the shoulder. "Aren't we're fortunate? After twelve condemnations, Kirral must be looking for a case where he can be generous, don't you think?" The cheer in his voice did not sound convincing.

DEAR READER

I hope you've enjoyed this book and gained many practical ideas for your writing. If you found it helpful, I'll be thrilled if you post a review on Amazon, Barnes&Noble, GoodReads, or wherever you purchased it or are a member.

If you email me the URL to your review, I'll send you a review ebook of one of my other Writer's Craft titles: *Writing Fight Scenes, Writing about Magic, The Word-Loss Diet, Writing Scary Scenes, Writing About Magic, Writing Dark Stories, Twitter for Writers, Writing Vivid Settings, Why Does My Book Not Sell? 20 Simple Fixes, Writing Short Stories To Promote Your Novels, Getting Book Reviews, How To Train Your Cat To Promote Your Book, Writing Deep Point of View, Writing Vivid Settings.* Email me which book you would like to review, *and I'll send it to you free.*

Let me know if you've found any errors, omissions, broken links or typos in this book, please let me know. Some errors always sneak past the eagle eyes of the proofreaders. Also contact me if you have questions. My email is *raynehall00000@gmail.com*. I look forward to hearing from you.

Perhaps you know other writers who might benefit from this book? Tell them about it.

On Twitter, you can follow me @RayneHall. *https://twitter.com/RayneHall* I'm very active on Twitter; it's my preferred social network. If you tweet that you've read this book, I'll follow you back – though you may have to remind me, because I have many followers and it's easy to miss a tweet.

Do you want to be the first to find out about new releases, special offers, contests and events? Sign up here to get my newsletter: *http://eepurl.com/boqJzD*.

Rayne Hall

Made in the USA
Las Vegas, NV
04 April 2022

46830402R00046